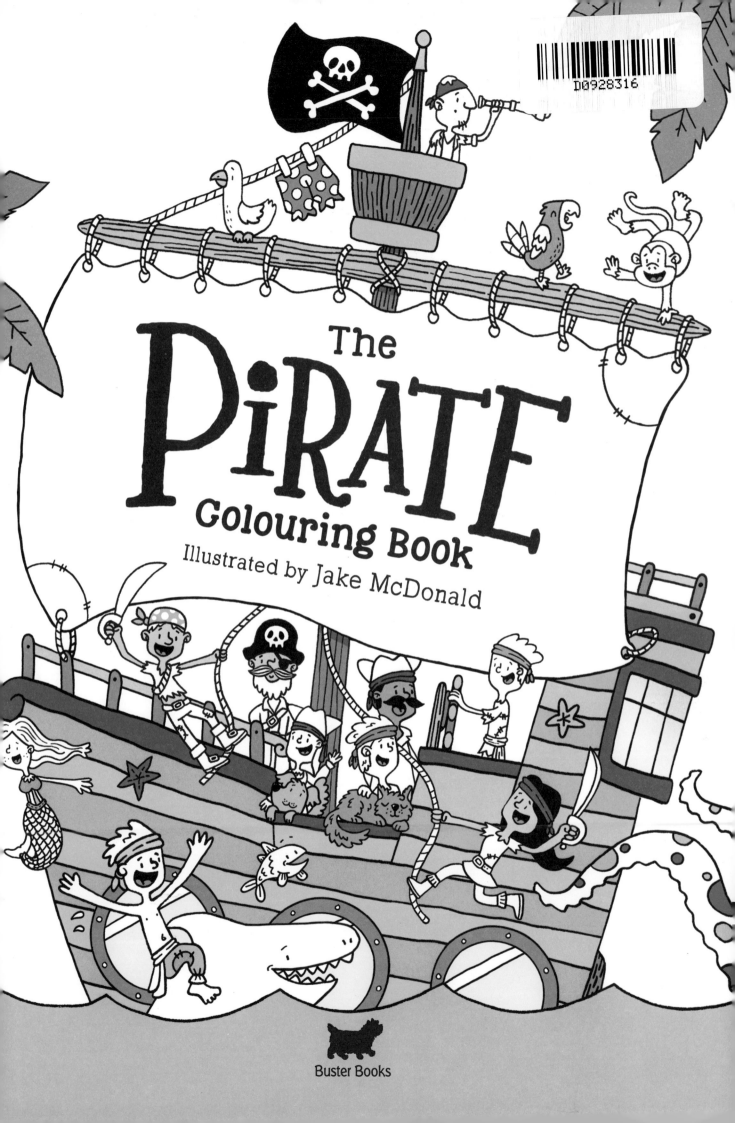

The PiRATE Colouring Book

Illustrated by Jake McDonald

Buster Books

This book was
coloured and
completed by

....

Chock full of treasure.

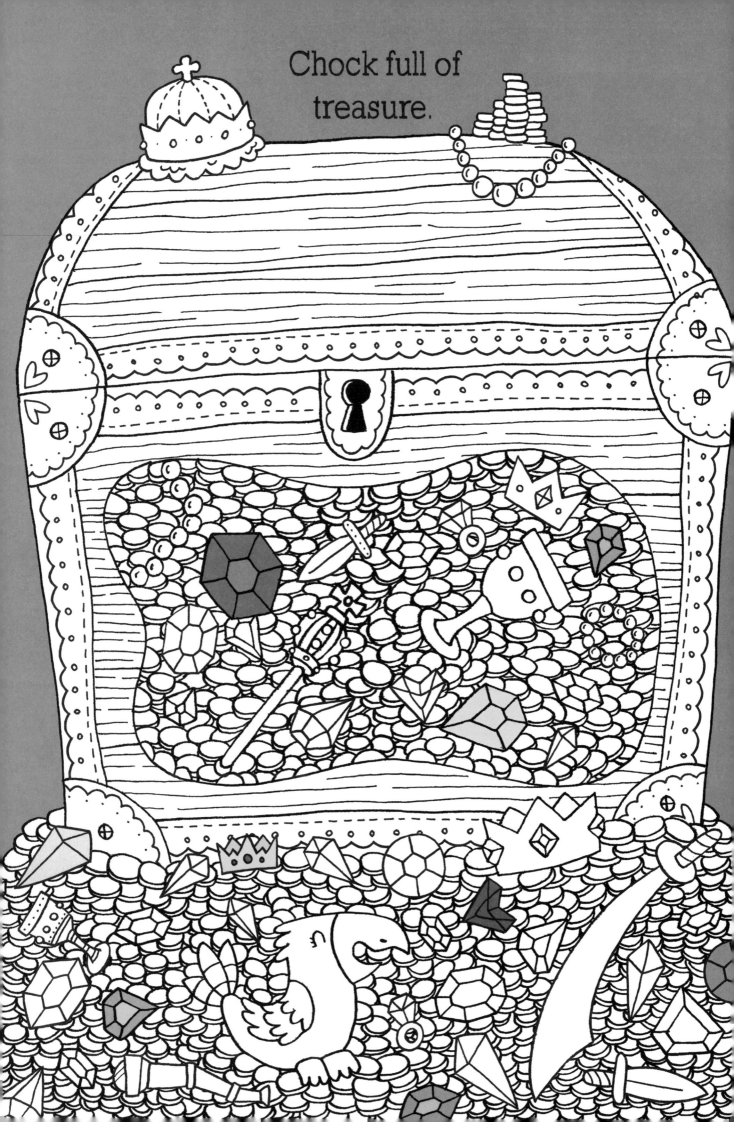

Can ye see inside
the barrels?

Where's the booty?

Welcome to the Captain's quarters.

First published in Great Britain in 2015 by
Buster Books, an imprint of Michael O'Mara Books Limited,
9 Lion Yard, Tremadoc Road, London SW4 7NQ

W www.busterbooks.co.uk f Buster Children's Books 🐦 @BusterBooks

ISBN: 978-1-78055-310-8

2 4 6 8 10 9 7 5 3 1

This book was printed in December 2014 by
Shenzhen Wing King Tong Paper Products Co. Ltd., Shenzhen, Guangdong, China.